© 1995 Royal Smeets Offset bv

Editions of this book will appear simultaneously in France, Great Britain, Italy and the Netherlands under the auspices of Euredition bv, Den Haag, Netherlands

This edition published by Magna Books, Magna Road, Wigston, Leicester LE18 4ZH, England

ISBN 1 85422 888 9

Translation: Tony Langham
Typesetting: Zspiegel grafische zetterij, Best
Printed in The Netherlands by Royal Smeets Offset, Weert

Production: VBI/SMEETS
Compilation: BoekBeeld, Utrecht
Design and text of plan, planting plan, flowering and colour scheme: Bureau Willemien Dijkshoorn BNT, Amsterdam
Editor A-Z: Yvonne Taverne, Utrecht
Editor-in-chief: Suzette E. Stumpel-Rienks, Bennekom
Photographs: Plant Pictures World Wide, Haarlem
Planning and maintenance, text: Suzette E. Stumpel-Rienks, Bennekom;
Drawings: Theo Schildkamp, Haaksbergen
Small workers in the garden, text and drawings: Theo Schildkamp, Haaksbergen

This edition has been compiled with the greatest possible care. Neither the compiler nor the editor accepts any liability for any damage as a result of possible inaccuracies and/or omissions in this edition.

Ferns for Home and Garden

Flowers & Plants

MAGNA BOOKS

Contents

Index   6

Introduction   7

Plan   8

Planting plan   9

A - Z of selected plants   10

Survey of garden and indoor ferns   72

Planting and Maintenance   74

Buying tips   75

Small workers in the garden   76

List of symbols   78

Index

Beech fern, Thelypteris 68
Bladder fern, Cystopteris 29
Bracken, Pteridium 64
Buckler fern, Dryopteris 36
Curly fern, Nephrolepis 42
Hart's tongue, Phyllitis 53
Hart's-horn fern, Platycerium 57
Iron fern, Cyrtomium 28
Japanese bird nest fern, Asplenium 15
Lady fern, Athyrium 19
Maidenhair fern, Adiantum 11
Marsh fern, Athyrium 19
Monkey's-foot fern, Davallia 30
Oak fern, Gymnocarpium 38
Pillwort, Pilularia 56
Polypody, Polypodium 60
Royal fern, Osmunda 47
Rusty-back fern, Ceterach 23
Shield fern, Polystichum 62
Spleenwort, Asplenium 14
Tree fern, Cyathea 26

Introduction

Beauty in the home and garden

Approximately 10,000 varieties of ferns are still growing on our planet, of which 3/4 are in tropical areas. In the vicinity of the equator, on the misty, forested slopes, these plants flourish in abundance. In the temperate regions there are c. 1,500 indigenous varieties. Of all these ferns, around 200-300 varieties are available on a regular basis. The most popular for the home and garden are even available throughout the year.

Ferns are unusual plants of great beauty. In the way they grow and propagate, they distinguish themselves from most other plants. Ferns do not blossom and propagate by means of spores. Their remarkable sex life is explained later in this book. And they are definitely fertile. Since they came into being (350 million years ago) they have conquered all continents. Of the original varieties, few have stood the ravages of time.

Tree ferns - the largest ferns known to be still in existence - are in a way the descendants of the Fern (Carboniferous) Period. They can grow up to 15 m high, with a leaf spread of 5 m or more. There are a few cultivated varieties, considerably smaller.

Because of their large range there are numerous species, not only water and desert ferns, but also climbing and arctic ferns. A fern can be made to feel at home in every corner of the house or garden.

Healthy ferns exude a natural beauty, peace and harmony - as every fern lover will agree.

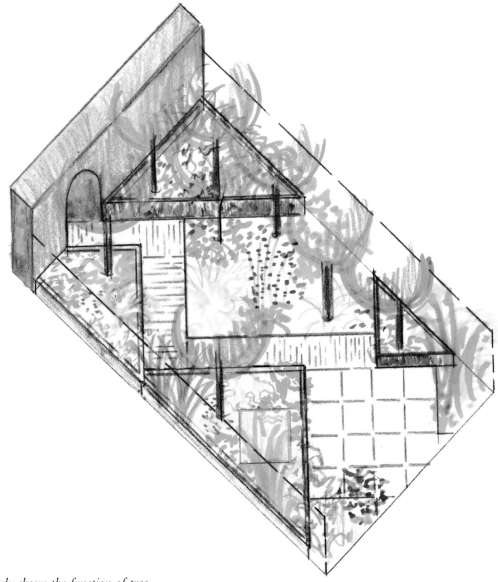

This sketch clearly shows the function of tree foliage. A shady atmosphere is created, which protects against direct light and oncoming winds.

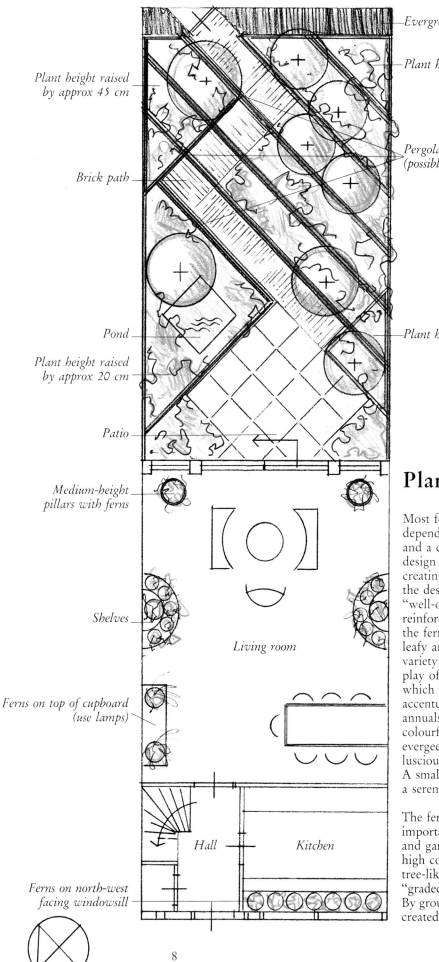

Evergreen hedge

Plant height raised by approx 55 cm

Plant height raised by approx 45 cm

Pergola
(possibly with hanging baskets)

Brick path

Plant height raised by approx 30 cm

Pond

Plant height raised by approx 20 cm

Patio

Medium-height pillars with ferns

Shelves

Ferns on top of cupboard
(use lamps)

Ferns on north-west facing windowsill

Living room

Hall

Kitchen

Plan

Most ferns are moisture-loving plants and depend on sufficient atmospheric humidity and a damp soil for a healthy existence. The design and spatial arrangement aim at creating a mysterious and shady effect. With the design of the garden on a diagonal, a "well-organised" effect is created. This is reinforced by the different levels at which the ferns are planted. The trees provide a leafy and shaded environment, and the variety of crown shapes creates a changing play of light and shade. A pergola from which baskets of ferns can be hung accentuates the shaded effect. Flowering annuals can be added to create a more colourful effect. The walls, covered in evergeen climbers, contribute to the luscious, green atmosphere - even in winter. A small pond, surrounded by ferns, provides a serene focal point.

The fern garden continues indoors - important for the perspective. Where house and garden meet, two ferns are placed on high columns, which gives them an almost tree-like function. In the room, ferns are "graded" on the shelves against the walls. By grouping several ferns, a green oasis is created which is worth every bit of attention.

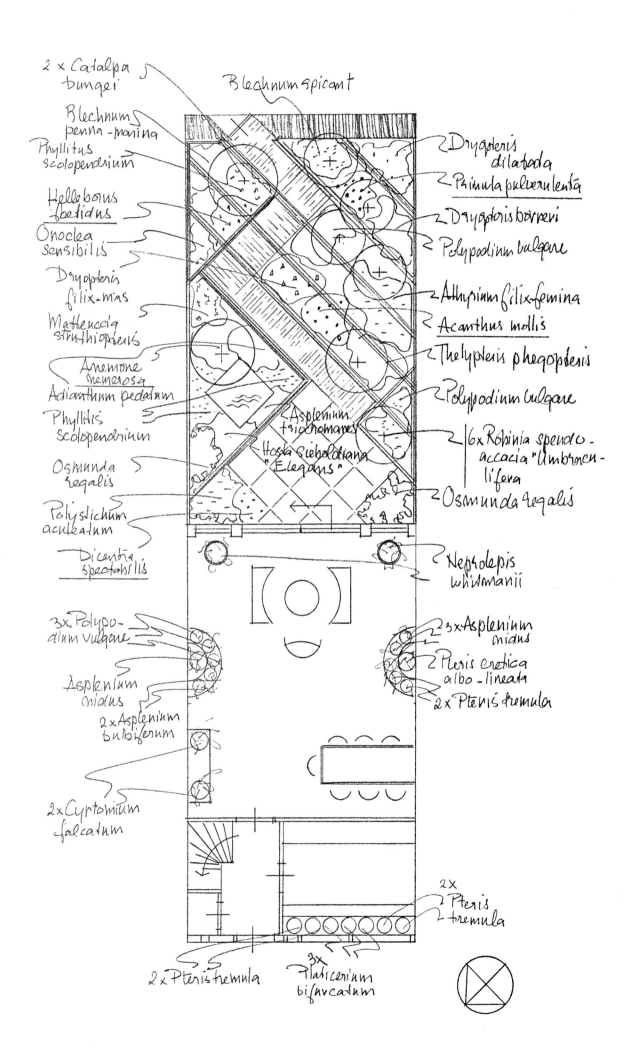

2 x Catalpa bungei

Blechnum spicant

Blechnum penna-marina

Phyllitis scolopendrium

Helleborus foetidus

Onoclea sensibilis

Dryopteris filix-mas

Matteuccia struthiopteris

Anemone nemerosa

Adianthum pedatum

Phyllitis scolopendrium

Osmunda regalis

Polystichum aculeatum

Dicentra spectabilis

3 x Polypodium vulgare

Asplenium nidus

2 x Asplenium bulbiferum

2 x Cyrtomium falcatum

Dryopteris dilatata

Primula pulverulenta

2 Dryopteris borreri

Polypodium vulgare

2 Athyrium filix-femina

Acanthus mollis

2 Thelypteris phegopteris

2 Polypodium vulgare

6 x Robinia spseudo-accacia "Umbraculifera"

2 Osmunda regalis

Nephrolepis whitmanii

Asplenium trichomanes

Hosta sieboldiana "Elegans"

3 x Asplenium nidus

2 Pteris cretica albo-lineata

2 x Pteris tremula

2 x Pteris tremula

2 x Pteris tremula

3 x Platicerium bifurcatum

Adiantum pedatum, Northern maidenhair fern

Adiantum
Maidenhair fern

◎ ↕ 15-50

Adiantum means "does not retain moisture", and this refers to the fact that when the leaves are sprayed, they do not retain any moisture. The genus comprises more than 200 species and is found throughout the world in tropical and subtropical regions, though mainly in the humid rainforests of Central and South America. A number of species are suitable for garden or pot plants. They are elegant, dainty ferns with composite, delicate pinnate leaves on strong, wiry, shiny, almost black stems. In general the spores are located on the edges of the leaves.

The winter-hardy species for the garden do very well in sheltered, shady spots, in moist, slightly acid soil, rich in humus. They look best in small groups. Plant rootstocks in shallow soil, and press down the soil evenly. Propagate from cuttings.

A. capillus-veneris, Maidenhair fern, is not really winter-hardy, though it can grow wild on walls and the sides of canals. It forms dainty, hanging fronds, consisting of 15-50 cm long, oval, evergreen, pinnate leaves with numerous triangular to oval leaflets on thin black stems. Add some lime to the soil.

A. pedatum (Northern maidenhair fern) has a creeping rootstock and dark stems which form clumps. It has round or horseshoe-shaped, delicate, parted leaves, 20-40 cm long. The young leaves turn from green to bluish-green; "Japonicum" has beautiful pink fronds in spring, which gradually turn pale green.

A. venustum is not entirely winter-hardy, and is a dense, creeping fern; it has black stems, and light green fronds, 15-25 cm long. The dead fronds are a beautiful brown colour and are not shed until the new leaves develop.

Indoors the ferns require a draught-free spot, not too much light, a minimum temperature of 18° C. and high humidity. The soil in the pot should always be fairly moist and should never be allowed to dry out. Water regularly and immerse the plant once a week. Water runs off the woody roots and is not absorbed, so that a clump of roots in the pot cannot retain much water and it is difficult to get it moist again once it has dried out. You can spray the plant or use the saucer method in order to achieve the required humidity. For the saucer method, place the plant on an upturned saucer in a dish of water. During the growth period from March to August,

top: Adiantum pedatum, Northern maidenhair fern
bottom: Adiantum pedatum, "Japonicum", Northern maidenhair fern

Adiantum hispidulum,
Maidenhair fern

Adiantum

feed once a fortnight with a low
concentration solution of nutrients -
approximately one-third of the
recommended amount.

Repot if necessary, preferably in spring in
ready-made soil for ferns, rich in humus, or
in a mixture of two parts potting compost
to one part peat and one part sharp sand,
and some rotted cow manure. If the leaves
have dried out, cut the stems above the
ground; when the old foliage has been cut
away, the plant may start to develop again
after resting for one or two months with
less water. The easiest way to propagate the
plant is to divide the rootstocks in the
spring and repot in small pots.

⬍ 30-75 🌡 ✂

A. hispidulum (syn. *A. pubescens*) is a short,
indoor fern with coarse hairs, and
greenish-bronze pinnate leaves on a sturdy
stem, 15-30 cm long. The plant grows best
in a temperate climate. It grows quickly,
keeps well, and can be incorporated in
mixed arrangements.

Adiantum cuneatum
"Fritz-Luthi",
Maidenhair fern

12

A. peruvianum is a fairly unusual indoor fern, with strong, slightly leathery leaves, 25-40 cm long, and wedge-shaped leaves with a broad, slightly lobed base.

A. raddianum (syn. *A. cuneatum*), an indoor fern, has tripinnate or quadripinnate curving leaves, 30 cm long. The small leaves are clearly wedge-shaped at the base, and there are three to six kidney-shaped sori along the edge of every leaf. There are quite a lot of cultivars: "Brilliant Else" grows profusely with greenish or golden-yellow leaves with a pinkish tinge; "Fragrans" has pale green leaves; "Fragrantissimum", 75 cm, has a fragrant smell; "Fritz-Luthi" is more erect with stiffer, darker leaves; "Glorytas" has bronze-coloured leaves. This Adiantum was originally grown in unheated greenhouses. It requires a high humidity level and can be used in arrangements of different plants.

A. tenerum is a species often cultivated in heated greenhouses. It has delicate tripinnate or quadripinnate leaves, 40 cm long, and thin, hard, dark brown stems. The stems of the leaves are broader at the top. The cultivars are stronger and more suitable for indoors: the young leaves of "Scutum Rosea" are pink, but turn green when the plant is mature. It should be placed in a fairly warm, extremely humid place.

Adiantum "Monocolor" is a species between *A. tenerum* and *A. raddianum*. It grows in a different way and has different shaped leaves. The irregular, overlapping leaves are densely packed on the stems. The young leaves do not have a pink or bronze colour. The foliage of *Adiantum* "Bronze Venus" is a bronze colour when it is young. The plant requires a fairly warm spot with high humidity.

Adiantum tenerum, Maidenhair fern

13

Asplenium
Spleenwort

⊘ ↕ 5-45

The name "Asplenium" is derived from the Greek words "a" (not) and "splen" (spleen), referring to the fact that the leaves are used as a remedy for spleen disorders. There are more than 600 species throughout the world. Most are indigenous in the rainforests of Asia, Africa and Australia. A number are epiphytic plants and grow on trees, collecting food in funnel-shaped rosettes of leaves. Others grow as ground cover in moist, shady soil. The often leathery, shiny, light or dark green leaves can be unparted, finely parted or pinnate. Some species are found in rocky regions and on old walls in western Europe. These are suitable for rockeries. Others are grown in conservatories or as pot plants.

This is an evergreen fern, so plant shallowly in the garden in lime-rich soil, preferably in a spot near to a fissure (walls).

Asplenium trichomanes, "Incisum", Spleenwort

14

A. adiantum-nigrum, black spleenwort, is found occasionally in this country on old walls. It has long, dark brown or black stems and bipinnate leaves with larger leaflets at the bottom, so that the whole leaf has a long, triangular shape. The sturdy, almost leathery leaf grows to a length of 10-45 cm; the long, narrow sori are in the middle of the leaves. This is a suitable plant for rockeries and walls, in shady spots in well-drained soil with some leaf-mould.
A. marinum, sea spleenwort, a rock plant from western England and western France with narrow, shiny, indented leaves, 10-40 cm long, purplish-brown stems and

long, narrow sori. Suitable for growing in cool spots and unheated greenhouses.
A. ruta-muraria, wall rue, is generally found on walls, in shady places along canals and waterways, in caves or on rocks, though it can also grow in slightly sunnier spots. It has an irregular shape, the leaves are 2-15 cm long and grow at an angle, often with trifoliate leaflets; it has thin, almost green leaf stems and long, thin sori.

*Asplenium antiquum,
Japanese bird nest fern*

Asplenium australasicum

A. septentrionale, forked spleenwort, grows in full sunlight on walls and rocky places. It has narrow, forked leaves, 5-20 cm long, and wedge-shaped leaflets; long, narrow sori.
A. trichomanes, maidenhair spleenwort, grows both in the shade and in full sunlight, in stony soil and on old walls. It has narrow pinnate leaves, 4-35 cm long, which grow rather flat against the ground; there are sturdy, dark green, oval, finely serrated leaflets on shiny, dark brown stems, and long, narrow sori. This elegant fern can also grow in dry, light places, but it requires a great deal of moisture in the sun. It may be necessary to add lime to the soil.
A. viride, green spleenwort, is very similar to *A. trichomanes*. It has fresh green stems and fronds, 6-20 cm long. It requires moist, lime-rich soil.
Asplenium species which are available as pot plants require a shady spot, extremely high humidity, and a minimum temperature of 18-22° C., 16° C. at night, and 12° C. in winter. The soil used in the pots should consist of equal parts of potting compost, sharp sand, peat or leaf-mould, and some bonemeal. During the growth period the

fern must be watered regularly and immersed from time to time. To achieve the necessary humidity, spray frequently with tepid water and place the plant on an upturned saucer in a dish of water. For the rest of the time the soil should be kept moderately moist. Dust the leaves and feed with a normal concentration of nutrient solution, once a fortnight. Propagate from spores (March to July/August), or if present, by removing bulbils with their roots.
A. antiquum, Japanese bird nest fern is a pot plant with narrow, single, undulating, pointed leaves which grow in rosettes. "Osaka" is a striking cultivar with shiny green leaves.
A. daucifolium has short leaf stems, delicate bipinnate or tripinnate leaves, 60 cm long and 20 cm wide, with small bulbils on the older leaves from which new ferns quickly develop.

A. nidus, Bird's nest fern, can grow to a fairly large size. It forms funnel-shaped rosettes of large, single, shiny, fresh green leaves up to 100 cm long, which have a dark brown central vein. The sori are located on the side veins of the older leaves. "Crispum" has unparted leaves with strongly undulating edges; "Fimbriatum" has deeply indented leaves. When the leaf turns brown along the edges, cut it away (without cutting the green part). Spray more frequently and feed with manure.

Asplenium antiquum "Osaka", Japanese bird nest fern

Asplenium australasicum "Crispum", Bird nest fern

17

Athyrium
Lady fern

◍ ◉ ↕ 80 ✳

Athyrium is found throughout the world. Most of the 200 species are indigenous in the temperate regions of the northern hemisphere. *A. filix-femina* is a common wild fern in humid woodlands and in shady spots along ditches and canals, sometimes growing in walls. It is also very popular as an ornamental plant.

This is an ornamental fern that is easy to grow, with pinnate, bipinnate or tripinnate leaves. It is extremely suitable for growing in shady spots in the garden, amongst ground cover, for planting under trees and shrubs and by the water's edge. It can tolerate some sunlight and requires normal, moist, slightly acid garden soil, rich in humus. Propagate from cuttings.

A. distentifolium (syn. *A. alpestre*), 80 cm, is widespread in France. It has green leaf stems, pale green, extremely pinnate leaves and round sori. *A. filix-femina*, lady fern, often grows higher, and has yellowish stems which are elegantly curved, bipinnate leaves which grow close together in groups, and long, narrow, hook-shaped sori in the shape of a comma. There are a large number of cultivars, including *A. filix-femina* "Cristatum", which has comb-shaped, branching leaves at the top; "Frizeliae", which has long, narrow leaves and half-moon-shaped terminal leaves; "Victoriae", 70-90 cm, has whorls of long, narrow, lanceolate to triangular fronds, crested (forming the "V" of Queen Victoria), pale green or light red, smooth stems; the leaves turn from a yellowish-green to a dark green.

A. nipponicum var. *Pictum* (syn. *A. goeringianum* "Pictum", a splendid, bushy, low fern from Japan, has slender, reddish stems, bipinnate, pyramidical leaves with long stems, and greyish-green leaflets with reddish veins. Grow in a sheltered spot.

top: Athyrium filix-femina, Lady fern

bottom: Athyrium nipponicum

left: Athyrium distentifolium, Lady fern

Blechnum

⊘ ◉ ↕ 15-65

There are approximately 200 *Blechnum*
varieties, mainly in the tropical and
subtropical regions of the southern
hemisphere. A few species are indigenous in
the northern hemisphere, including
B. spicant, hard fern, which can be found in
the Netherlands in acid soil lacking in
nutrition, in moist, deciduous and
coniferous woodlands, by ditches and
canals, inland dunes and on a number of
islands in the Wadden Sea.
In some species the rootstock forms a sort
of trunk as the plant develops. The rather
leathery leaves are usually pinnate; the
fertile leaves have long, narrow sori at the
back. They often differ from the sterile
(infertile) leaves.
A number of varieties are suitable for
growing in the garden or can survive
indoors for a long time if properly cared
for.
Garden ferns require acid, moist soil lacking

Blechnum penna-marina

Blechnum gibbum

in nutrients and may have to be covered in winter (*B. penna-marina*). Do not remove dead leaves until the young fronds appear in spring. They tolerate fairly dry air. Propagate from spores and cuttings.

B. penna-marina, 15-30 cm, is not really winter-hardy in colder regions. It is a creeping fern suitable for ground cover and the yellowish green, stiffly pinnate leaves grow up and curve. Suitable for rockeries.

P. spicant, hard fern, has two distinct sorts of leaves: the hanging or horizontal sterile leaves forming a rosette on the ground, and the erect, fertile leaves, which are longer and have very narrow leaflets like a herring-bone. This evergreen fern is suitable for growing wild and in rockeries and thrives in moist shady spots, e.g., under shrubs.

Indoor ferns require a light warm spot, 16-24° C, 14° C in winter. Do not place in direct sunlight. The soil must be rich in humus, well-drained and not too heavy. (e.g., equal parts of potting compost, sharp sand, peat or leaf-mould and some bonemeal); the plant should not stand in water, though the humidity must be fairly high. You could use the saucer method or spray lightly. The soil must be kept fairly moist at all times and should never be allowed to dry out. During the growing period water amply at regular intervals and feed once a month (half concentration). Remove dead fronds; water on the leaves results in black patches. Repot in spring when there are too many roots. Propagate from spores and cuttings.

⬆ 100 🍺 ✂

B. brasiliense becomes fairly large as an indoor plant. It grows rapidly, forming a trunk with fibrous dark-brown scales. The pinnate, slightly leathery leaves are arranged in compact rosettes, partly overlapping. The leaves are reddish-brown when they are young and later turn dark green.

B. gibbum also becomes fairly large, but grows more slowly. It has a black, scaly trunk with large, funnel-shaped, shiny, pale green leaves with a single indentation and narrow, pointed leaflets arranged in compact, regular rosettes. The fertile leaves are narrower and more curved than the sterile leaves.

Blechnum spicant

Ceterach
Rusty-back fern

○ ◉ ↕ 20 ✳

Ceterach, which is also available under the name *Asplenium*, comprises three very similar species and is found in Europe, Africa and Asia. Like many ferns, it grows in rock fissures and old walls (though it is very rare in our part of the world), but in contrast with most ferns it tolerates dry conditions very well and likes open, fairly sunny spots; in fact, the leaves actually wilt if there is too much shade.

This is a small fern with short straight rootstocks, thick lanceolate, deeply lobed leaves with scales on the underside and long, narrow sori on the central veins of the leaf lobes.

The rusty-back fern prefers rock fissures, but is also suitable in rockeries. It requires a calcareous, rather loamy, lime-rich soil, which is always moist. Alternating dry and wet soil can be very bad for the plant. Propagate by (carefully) dividing the rootstock.

Ceterach officinarum,
Rusty-back fern

Ceterach officinarum, Rusty-back fern

C. *officinarum* (syn. *Asplenium ceterach*) is sometimes found in this part of the world on old chalky walls. It is fairly winter-hardy, with deeply indented leaves with long stems, 5-20 cm long, and broad, blunt, alternating lobes which are a dull greyish-green and bare at the top, with shiny silver scales, later turning brown, at the bottom. In dry periods the leaves curl so that the plant looks rather dried out. As soon as there is any rain they open up again as though nothing was the matter at all.

side with thick, shiny, white hair on the underside. When it is dry the leaves curl round; when it has rained they unfurl again. *C. pterichoides*, has bipinnate, reddish, scaly, fragrant leaves, 10-30 cm long.

Cheilanthes spec.

Cheilanthes

◎ ↕ 30

Cheilanthes is a widespread genus. There are approximately 180 species, which are found both in hot and temperate regions. Most are tropical, but a few are winter-hardy.
This is a small evergreen fern with bipinnate or multipinnate, pronounced, parted leaves with stems. They are often hairy or covered in scales on both sides, but mainly on the underside.
Suitable for rockeries in sheltered spots in arid well-drained soil that is not too wet; do not give too much water and protect in winter if necessary; feed once every two months in the growing season (spring, summer) with a half concentration.
Propagate by dividing rootstock.
C. lanosa has a slightly creeping rootstock, hairy stems, bipinnate yellowish or bluish-green leaves, 15-30 cm long, lobed at the end. There are pairs or alternating oval pinnate leaflets, slightly hairy on the upper

Cibotium schiedei

Cibotium

⊘ ⇅ 100-200 ▢

Cibotium is indigenous in the tropical
regions of Asia, Central America and
Oceania. It is a tree fern and can grow to a
height of 5 m in the country of origin; the
young cultivated specimens are usually
much lower and often have no trunk. In
this case the fronds grow directly from the
ground. The long, silky hairs which are
found on the trunk and fronds are
sometimes used to staunch blood (China) or
as stuffing for cushions (Hawaii). This is a
large, elegant fern with a fibrous, hairy
trunk and large, long, triangular, bipinnate
or tripinnate leaves at the top.
As an indoor fern it is suitable for growing
in tubs in large rooms in light or shady
spots, sheltered from direct sunlight. The
soil should be moist and well-drained, e.g.,
a mixture of equal parts of potting compost,
sharp sand, leaf-mould or peat, with some
bonemeal. The level of moisture should be
constant, do not overwater (root rot). Water
less in winter; temperature in the day,
21-26° C; at night, 10-15° C. Feed once a
month during the growing period (spring to
summer) with half concentration. Repot if
necessary in early spring. The pot should
not be too large. Propagate from spores.
C. barometz has no trunk or a very short,
reddish-brown hairy trunk and leathery,
fragrant, hairy fronds, 1-1.5 m long.
C. glaucum, Hawaiian tree fern, has a
golden-brown, hairy trunk, wrinkled fronds
up to 2 m long and sickle-shaped leaves
without stems. The lower pair are lobed at
the base.
C. schiedei, Mexican tree fern, a cultivar, has
virtually no trunk. It has elegantly curved,
pale green fronds, bluish at the base, 1-1.5 m
long (in Mexico, up to 4.5 m long), which
grow in groups. The young stems are
yellowish-brown and hairy.

top and bottom: Cibotium schiedei

Cyathea
Tree fern

⊘ ↕ 200-300 🌡 ◁ (trunk)

Cyathea is indigenous in tropical and subtropical regions. These evergreen ferns have a very tall trunk covered with old leaf sheaths and aerial roots, and enormous, leathery, bipinnate or tripinnate parted or lobed, sometimes hairy leaves. Some species have spiny leaf stems and veins. In the place of origin the ferns can grow to an enormous size, but the cultivars grow more slowly and are not as large. In temperate regions they do best in a greenhouse or indoor office garden.
These plants are large even when cultivated; they require well-drained, nutritious soil which is always moist (e.g., equal parts of potting compost, leaf-mould or peat, sharp sand and some bonemeal). If the plant dries out, the leaves turn yellow. The trunk should be regularly sprayed. Feed once or twice during the growing season (half concentration). Place in a light place, but protect from direct sunlight. Temperature in the day, 21-26° C; at night, 18° C.
C. medullaris, approximately 14° C.

Remove dead fronds in winter. Propagate from spores.
C. australis (syn. *Alsophila australis*) can have a trunk 5-6 m tall in its country of origin (Australia), and gigantic fan-shaped fronds with a diameter of 6 m. Cultivated specimens are usually about 2-2.5 m tall. They have a dark, scaly trunk and stems and green tripinnate leaves which are sea-green at the base.
C. cooperi (syn. *Alsophila cooperi*) is similar to *C. australis*. It grows more rapidly and has shiny, scaly, brown stems and metallic green, delicately parted leaves.
C. medullaris (syn. *Sphaeropteris medullaris*) from New Zealand, can grow to a height of 10-20 m with a trunk 75 cm thick and gigantic fronds 2-6 m long and up to 1.5 m wide, which are pale green at the base and dark green at the top with black veins.

Cyathea cooperi

Cyathea species

Cyrtomium
Iron fern

⊘ ◉ ↕ 30-40 ▯ ✄

The name *Cyrtomium* comes from the Greek word kyrtos (curved) which refers to the slightly sickle-shaped, curved leaves. This fern is widespread and is indigenous in China, Africa and Hawaii, amongst other places. It is an extremely strong fern which requires very little light as long as the temperature is not too high. In hotter regions it thrives in the open ground in moist, shady spots. In this part of the world it is occasionally found growing wild on walls.

This fern has short, flaky rootstocks, pinnate, serrated or smooth leaves, with broad, sickle-shaped leaflets and sori spread over the entire underside of the leaf.

It is a strong plant, easy to grow indoors in porous, slightly moist soil, rich in humus (equal parts of potting compost, peat, sharp sand and some bonemeal). Water generously in summer, spray regularly, immerse once a month. Feed regularly (one third of the concentration). Temperature during the day, 16-20° C; at night, 10-12° C. Allow the plant to rest in winter in a cooler spot (7-10° C, with less water). Repot plants in spring when the roots have become too compacted. Propagate from spores and cuttings.

C. falcatum (syn. *Aspidium falcatum, Polystichum falcatum*) has hairy stems with brown scales at the base, leathery, shiny, dark green pinnate leaves with whorls of short-stemmed, serrated leaves, smooth at the top. *C. falcatum* "Roch-fordii" (syn. *C. rochfordianum*) has broader, fairly deeply and irregularly indented leaves. The numerous spores on the underside of the leaves can look like a layer of rust and can fall en masse, making rather a mess.

C. fortunei (syn. *Polystichum fortunei*) has brownish, scaly stems, slightly broader, matt green pinnate leaves with a large number of lanceolate or sickle-shaped serrated leaflets.

top: Cyrtomium cliviola, Iron fern
bottom: Cyrtomium Falcatum, Iron fern

Cystopteris
Bladder fern

◉ ⤒ 10-60

Cystopteris is indigenous in the temperate regions of the northern hemisphere. The 19 different species grow on shady, rocky slopes and old, damp walls; *C. fragilis* is occasionally found in this part of the world, and because it is so rare, it should certainly not be removed. It is a delicate, airy fern with dainty, deeply indented fronds and sori which look like bladders on the underside of the leaves.

These ferns are suitable for rockeries, shady, moist spots, and damp cavities in old walls. Cultivate in a mixture of leaf-mould, loam, sharp sand and some ground lime.

Propagate by dividing the clumps in spring. *C. bulbifera* can also be propagated by removing and planting out the bulbils.

C. bulbifera has curved fronds 30-60 cm long, with partly overlapping leaflets close together. In addition to the sori, it develops bulbils from which new plants may develop in the autumn.

C. dickiana, Dickie's bladder fern, is very similar to *C. bulbifera*, but has smaller, overlapping fronds.

C. filix-fragilis, brittle bladder fern, (syn. *Cystopteris fragilis*), has short, scaly rootstocks and dark, brittle stems, 10-40 cm long, with bipinnate fronds arranged close together, about halfway up. The lower pair of leaflets is usually shorter than the other leaflets. It is sensitive to dry conditions. The foliage starts to die off in winter.

C. montana, mountain bladder fern, has long, creeping rootstocks, and triangular fronds, 10-30 cm long; each lower pair of leaflets is longer than the next pair.

Cystopteris bulbifera,
Bladder fern

Davallia
Monkey's-foot fern

⬤ ↧ 30-85 ▽ ✂

Davallia is mainly indigenous in the tropical regions of Asia, and some species grow in Morocco, the Iberian peninsula and the Canary Islands. It is an epiphytic plant, which means that it roots on parts of other plants, though unlike parasitic plants it does not extract nutrients from them. There are approximately 40 species which have creeping, scaly, hairy rootstocks. In plant pots and hanging baskets, these grow over the edges. The leaves are pinnate or multi-pinnate and the sori are along the edges of the leaves. The old fronds do not die off until the new young fronds are fairly large.

This is an indoor fern for a light or shady spot. It should be protected from the sun. It requires porous soil, rich in humus (equal parts of leaf-mould, peat, coniferous

Davallia canariensis,
Monkey's-foot fern

Davallia solida

woodland soil and some sharp sand.) Keep moist. If necessary, put it on an upturned saucer in a dish of water, and immerse from time to time. Approximately 20-24° C. in the day, 7-15° C. at night. Feed once every two/three weeks during the growing period (half of the prescribed concentration). Remove faded leaves in winter. Repot plants in spring when they become too large. Propagate by dividing the rootstock.

D. canariensis has creeping brown rootstocks with soft hairs, and triangular, deeply indented, parted, hairless leaves, 30-50 cm long, and 20-35 cm wide, with long stems.

D. divaricata has hairy rootstocks which bear some resemblance to a monkey's foot. It has bipinnate or tripinnate leaves, 50-85 cm long, with short stems.

D. mariesii (syn. *D. bullata*) has light brown, scaly, hairy rootstocks, and pale green, bipinnate leaves, 15-40 cm long, and almost as wide.

This is a medium to large fern which grows rapidly, forming dense vegetation with creeping rootstocks. It has hairy, bipinnate or tripinnate leaves with sori in the corners. This fern proliferates and has few requirements. It is suitable for growing in a shady spot in any moist, well-drained soil, e.g., a mixture of loam, sharp sand, leaf-mould or peat. Keep sufficiently moist in the sun. Do not remove the fronds which turn brown in autumn, until the new leaves develop (spring). Good ground cover. Propagate in spring by dividing rootstocks and from spores (at the end of the summer/autumn). It is possible to restrict the growth of the fern by placing a ring of stones in the soil.

D. cicutaria, an evergreen, has hairy, hanging fronds,100-200 cm long.

D. punctiloba (syn. *Dicksonia punctilobula*), has branching rootstocks and curved, oval, bipinnate, fresh green leaves, 30-90 cm long, covered with white hair on the underside; crushed leaves smell of freshly-mown hay.

Dennstaedtia

○ ◐ ● ↕ 30-200 ✳

Dennstaedtia is mainly indigenous in tropical and subtropical forests; some species are found in temperate regions. They are suitable for growing in the garden and are occasionally available as indoor plants.

Dennstaedtia punctiloba

Dicksonia

⌀ ↕ 100-200 🏺 ✂ (trunk)

Dicksonia is indigenous in mountainous regions of America, Australia and New Zealand, amongst other places. It has been classified as a tree fern, and can be cultivated in greenhouses and office gardens, like Cyathea, with which it is often confused. Like that fern, it can grow to a great height in the natural state; it is distinguished mainly by its bristly, hairy trunk.

The trunk of this tree fern actually consists of sturdy leaf stalks growing in a spiral, covered with remnants of the leaf sheaths, bristly hairs and rough, aerial roots growing close together. It has a broad crown of fronds consisting of large, stiff, bipinnate or tripinnate leaves with short stems which are lighter and hairier at the base. The sori are on the edges of the leaves.

These tree ferns are cultivated to a height of 1-2 m in a light place, protected from bright sunlight, in moist, very well-drained, nutritious soil (equal parts of potting compost, sharp sand, peat and some bonemeal). Water generously, slightly less in winter, spray the stem and feed once a month during the growing season (half concentration), and in spring and summer. Do not remove the leaf sheaths when the leaves have been shed. Only repot when the

Dicksonia antarctica

Dicksonia antarctica

roots become choked. Propagate from spores, or if possible, by carefully removing runners (with stem).

In its natural habitat, *D. antarctica* can grow to a height of 10-15 m, with leathery, dark green fronds, 2-2.5 m long, yellowish veins and hairy brown stems.

In warmer regions, *D. antarctica* can grow outdoors in light shade, in a warm, moist, sheltered spot.

D. fibrosa grows more slowly and does not grow as tall, up to 7 m, with dark green fronds approximately 1-1.5 m long, and black, hairy stems.

D. squarrosa grows to a height of 6 m. It develops a rather flat crown of horizontal, bright blue fronds, 50-120 cm long, and has a black, hairy trunk and stems. Smaller

trunks can grow from the runners to form a sort of cave-like structure with the main trunk. There are dormant buds on the trunk from which new plants frequently develop.

Dicksonia antarctica

Didymochlaena truncatula

Didymochlaena

⊘ ◉ ↕ 150-200 🍶 ✂

The name *Didymochlaena* is derived from the Greek words "didymos" (double) and "chlaina" (cloak), which refer to the shape of the covering of the sori. It is found in tropical regions throughout the world, and comprises only one species, *D. truncatula*. It was cultivated in England in 1838, and is now a common and popular potted plant. This is an easy plant to grow if it is placed in a warm, light spot, out of direct sunlight. It requires constantly moist soil, rich in humus (compost, leaf-mould or peat). It is very bad for the roots to become dry. Temperature, 20-22° C. Spray frequently, especially the young leaves. Feed once a month during the growing season (May-October) with a greatly diluted concentration. In the spring, repot plants which have grown considerably. This should be done very carefully, as the roots are delicate. Propagate from cuttings, damaging the roots as little as possible, and by sowing the spores.

D. truncatula (syn. *D. lunulata*) has erect stems with large, leathery, shiny, dark green bipinnate leaves and blunt, squarish leaves with slightly wavy edges, arranged close together. The young leaves have a slightly bronze colour. The five or six heaps of sori are along the outer edges.

Doryopteris

⌀ ↕ 30-70 ⊔

The name *Doryopteris* is derived from the Greek words "doris" (spear) and "pteris" (fern), referring to the shape of the leaves of several species. It is indigenous throughout the tropics and subtropics, mainly in Brazil. These are small or medium ferns with shiny, green stems which turn brown or black, and leathery, light or dark green, oval, spear-shaped or palmate leaves, with palmate lobes which may themselves be lobed or parted. The sori are on the edges of the leaves. The fertile fronds may differ from the infertile fronds.

If it is properly cared for, this attractive fern can survive indoors for many years. It should be placed in a light spot and protected from sunlight. It requires fairly moist, well-drained soil, rich in humus (equal parts of potting compost, leaf-mould, sharp sand, and some bonemeal). It should not be given too much water, and can be placed on an upturned saucer in a dish of water. Temperature, 24-26° C. in the daytime and 15-21° C. at night. Feed during the growing season, in spring and summer (half concentration).

Repot when the plant becomes too large. Propagate by sowing spores, or if possible, removing and potting young plants.

D. ludens is a creeping fern with black stems, palmate, lobed, fertile fronds, 50-70 cm long, and oval, spear-shaped or palmate, double-lobed infertile fronds, 30-50 cm long.

D. nobilis has deeply palmate, lobed, pinnate, fertile fronds, and heart-shaped or spear-shaped, less parted, infertile fronds, some of which have young plants by the stem.

D. pedata has short rootstocks, usually hairy stems, broad, lobed, pinnate, infertile fronds with short stems and palmate, parted or (double-)lobed fertile fronds with longer stems. *D. pedata* var. *palmata* (syn. *D. palmata*) has larger fronds; young plants may develop at the base of these.

Doryopteris pedata

Dryopteris
Buckler fern

◔ ◉ ↕ 30-150 ✳

Dryopteris is found virtually all over the world in both tropical and temperate zones, e.g., in Northern Europe and North America; some of the 150 species are also indigenous in this part of the world and are fairly common in deciduous and coniferous woodland in undergrowth, by ditches, and sometimes in reed beds. This genus of ferns has had several different names, for example, several species have been classified under *Thelypteris*.

This fern has a short, thick, scaly, brown rootstock and pinnate or bipinnate leaves with (short) stems often grouped together. In England many hybrids were developed with differently shaped leaves varying from narrow or broad, curling or frizzy leaves. These are woodland ferns for growing in light and dark spots, e.g., under conifers in moist soil, rich in humus. *D. filix-mas* "Cristata", crested buckler fern, requires damper soil. *D. carthusiana* and *D. dilatata* need a lot of leaf-mould and well-drained acid soil. Propagate by collecting and sowing the spores (May to October), or from cuttings of plants which are at least three years old (October to November). *D. carthusiana* (syn. *D. spinulosa*), narrow buckler fern, and *D. dilatata* (syn. *D. austriaca*), broad buckler fern, are very

Dryopteris affinis "Crispa"

Dryopteris filix-mas, Male fern

similar. The remaining ferns have triangular composite leaves. *D. carthusiana*, 30-90 cm, has pale green leaves on light brown, rather brittle, scaly stems which are almost as long; *D. dilatata* is taller, growing to a height of 150 cm with dark green leaves hanging at the top and short sturdy, dark, scaly stems. *D. cristata*, crested buckler fern, 45-80 cm, has a creeping rootstock, narrow, lanceolate, evergreen infertile fronds which spread out, and longer, erect, fertile fronds with slightly horizontally twisted leaves on yellowish, green stems. The fertile leaves die off at the end of the growing season. This fern is particularly suitable for marshy spots. *D. filix-mas*, the male fern, is very similar to the lady fern (*Athyrium filix-femina*), but is sturdier and the fronds are not so narrow at the base. It has a short rootstock, 30-120 cm long, covered with brown scales (sometimes used as a remedy for tape worms), with leathery pinnate leaves in compact, spiralling clusters on short, scaly, light brown stems. The infertile leaves are almost evergreen (in warmer regions they are completely evergreen); the fertile leaves die off after periods of frost. *D. filix-mas* "Crispa" has attractive, curling fronds; the leaves of "Cristata" have crested ends;

Dryopteris affinis

Dryopteris wallichiana

"Grandiceps" has bluish leaves with large crests at the ends.

D. goldiana, 100-150 cm, is not evergreen and has a short, creeping rootstock, compact groups of sturdy, leathery, pinnate, parted leaves, tightly grouped, pointed leaflets and scaly stems.

D. pseudomas (syn. *D. borreri*), the scaly male fern, 50-150 cm, with young, yellowish-green leaves which are serrated at the top, and bright orange scaly stems. The leaves remain on the fern during the winter, but die off at the end of the winter.

D. villarsii (syn. *D. rigida*), the rigid buckler fern, 20-60 cm, is an evergreen fern which grows in lime-rich, rocky soil, e.g., in the Alps and Pyrenees. It has aromatic fronds on thin stems of the same length which form a funnel; it is suitable for rockeries.

Gymnocarpium
Oak fern

◎ ⦿ ↕ 10-45 ✳

In the past, *Gymnocarpium* was classified under *Dryopteris*, and this genus is very similar. The five species are indigenous in the temperate zones of Europe, America and Asia; several can be found in this part of the world in shady spots, by ditches and canals, and sometimes on walls. This fern sheds its leaves and has a creeping branched rootstock with triangular, membranous fronds at (ir)regular distances, and round sori.

These are winter-hardy ferns for very shady spots, in the rockery or in a shady border. They require moist, loamy soal, rich in humus, mixed with leaf-mould and peat. Propagate by dividing the rootstocks or by sowing the spores.

G. dryopteris (syn. *Dryopteris linnaena*), the oak fern, has thin black rootstocks covered with brown flakes, delicate pale green, bipinnate or tripinnate leaves, 10-45 cm, long with lobed leaflets. The triangular to pentangular leaves are almost at right-angles to the stem.

G. robertianum (syn. *Dryopteris robertiana*), the limestone fern, has black rootstocks with a few light brown flakes. It has triangular, bipinnate leaves, 15-30 cm long, and feathery, lobed leaflets at the end of the stem. Both the stems and fronds are covered with small glands. This fern prefers lime-rich soil.

Gymnocarpium dryopteris, Oak fern

Humata tyermannii

Humata

⊘ ↕ 20-30 ⊎

Humata is indigenous in tropical Asia and Madagascar. It is closely related to *Davallia* and is occasionally mistakenly available under that name. The resemblance can be seen in the hairy, rootstocks which grow above the ground. There are 50 species and one of these, *H. tyermannii*, is cultivated as an indoor fern; it thrives in a pot or hanging basket. The hairy rootstocks will grow over the edges of the pot on all sides. This fern requires a light spot protected from the sun, moist soil rich in humus, e.g., a mixture of potting compost, sharp sand, peat or leaf-mould and some vermiculite. The soil must not be too moist or the rootstocks will turn brown, temperature by day 21-26° C, at night 10-15° C. Feed once a month (half concentration). Repot once every two/three years when the soil has been exhausted.

Propagate by dividing rootstocks.
H. tyermannii has fairly thick, creeping, thick, silvery-white rootstocks with short hair, with brownish-green stems developing every 5-8 cm, with leathery, triangular, parted leaves. The young leaves are reddish; the older leaves, dark green. This fern sheds its leaves, but in warm, humid conditions the old fronds remain on the plant until the new ones appear in the spring.

39

Matteuccia

○ ⊘ ◉ ⫼ 150 ✳

Matteuccia is indigenous in Central Europe (from the Ardennes) Northern Asia and North America . It is a spreading woodland fern which thrives in good soil when there is sufficient humidity, both in light shade and in the sun.

This fern has a creeping rootstock and clearly distinct fertile and infertile bipinnate leaves arranged in rings or groups.

This winter-hardy woodland fern can be grown individually or in groups by a pond or under trees, in nutritious moist soil, e.g., a mixture of loam, leaf-mould or peat. The sunnier the spot, the more moisture it requires. Young shoots can be removed to prevent the fern spreading. Ugly, infertile leaves can be removed in winter. Propagate by dividing rootstocks (spring).

M. pennsylvanica (syn. *M. struthiopteris* var. *pennsylvanica*), the American ostrich fern, can grow to a height of 6 m in its natural habitat (North America). When it is cultivated, the fronds, which grow in groups, do not grow so tall, up to 1.5 to 1.8 m. The leathery, dark green, broad, oval, pointed, infertile fronds develop first, surrounding the tough, brownish, fertile fronds which are half the size and develop

Matteuccia struthiopteris

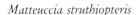

Matteuccia struthiopteris

Matteuccia struthiopteris

later in the summer, with tightly packed, very small leaflets. At the end of the summer the infertile fronds become rather ugly and turn brown in autumn; the brown, fertile fronds remain on the fern all winter. It does not develop as many runners as the next species and is therefore more suitable for smaller gardens, though it is one of the tallest garden ferns.

M. struthiopteris, the ostrich fern, 1-1.5 m, is very winter-hardy. It has a vertical rootstock which sometimes protrudes up to 10 cm above the ground. In spring, pale green, broad, pinnate, pointed infertile leaves curved at the top develop in rosettes with narrow pointed, wavy pinnate leaflets. In the summer, the narrower fertile leaves, which are half the size, develop in these with curling leaflets enclosing the sori on the underside. They start off a bronze colour and later turn rust-coloured. The fertile leaves remain on the plant in winter.

M. speluncae grows rapidly. It has a hairy pelleted seed, pale light green, bipinnate to quadripinnate leaves, 40-50 cm long and 20-30 cm wide, and indented leaflets with sori on the edges. The leaves of *M. speluncae* "Cristata" broaden out in a crest.

Microlepia

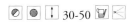 30-50

Microlepia species, indigenous in the tropical and subtropical regions of America, Africa and Asia, are elegant ferns, easy to grow in (sub)tropical woodland gardens; they are more difficult as indoor specimens and do not tolerate dry conditions very well. In general, they survive only for a year.
This is a medium to large fern with creeping rootstocks and closely packed, pale, bright green, pinnate or multi-pinnate leaves which are serrated at the ends. Indoors this fern should be placed in a slightly shady or even dark spot. It is suitable for plant boxes with nutritious soil, rich in humus, e.g., three parts of leaf-mould, two parts of well-rotted manure, one part of sharp sand. The soil should always be moist. Spray plant regularly. Water less in winter. During the growing season feed once a fortnight (normal concentration). Temperature 18-22° C, 15° C in winter. Repot every year in spring. Propagate by dividing and sowing spores.

Microlepia speluncae

41

Nephrolepis cordifolia, Curly fern

Nephrolepis
Curly fern

⊘ ◉ ↕ 30-70 ⏢ ✄

Nephrolepis is very common throughout the tropical and subtropical regions of the world and is one of the most common indoor ornamental ferns. In their natural habitat the plants are epiphytic ferns growing on trees, or simply in the soil, in compact groups with short stems and long, narrow, pinnate leaves. Cultivars may have multi-parted leaves which can be curly, frizzy or fringed.

These ferns actually belong in heated greenhouses, but are strong enough to survive indoors for some time. If they are repotted in spring every year and kept sufficiently moist, they can survive for several years. They can be placed in fairly light or darker spots out of direct sunlight. They require nutritious soil rich in humus, e.g., a mixture of peat or leaf-mould, sharp sand, vermiculite and some bonemeal. Maintain an even level of humidity, spray regularly and feed regularly during the growing season when watering the plant (half concentration). Do not feed in winter or during a rest period. Temperature 18-22° C, winter minimum 18° C. Repot every year in spring. Cut away fronds when they have turned yellow and replace runners in the soil or cut away. A fern which is no longer attractive can look better when the old yellow leaves have been removed. Place the plant in a cooler place (about 5 degrees lower), and water less; repot after one to two months and try to encourage growth in a warmer spot. Propagate from spores (wild species), by removing runners and by carefully dividing, damaging the roots as little as possible.

N. cordifolia (syn. *N. cordata*) has shiny, dark, slightly scaly stems, 5-8 cm long, erect pinnate leaves, 30-60 cm long and 4-6 cm wide, with closely packed lobed, leaflets and sori close to the edge. It forms many runners with small bulbils. *N. cordifolia* "Plumosa" has darker green leaves and the leaflets are pinnate at the top; it also forms runners with bulbils.

N. duffi (syn. *N. cordifolia* "Duffi"), has erect, very narrow leaves which curl or fork at the ends with small, oval to round leaflets; it does not develop spores.

N. exaltata has bare green stems, or the stems are covered with very light greyish hairs, and erect stiff leaves, 60-70 cm long and 6-15 cm wide, with closely packed long leaflets on the stem and sori along the edge. There are many cultivars available of this species; they are distinguished by their pinnate or multipinnate leaves. Varieties with single pinnate leaves include "Atlanta" with erect yellowish-green fronds, "Boston Marathon", a compact fern with broad fronds and wavy leaflets; "Bostoniensis" which has broad, dark-green, hanging fronds and wavy leaflets; there are many cultivars of this variety with delicate wrinkled and crested fronds; "Maassii", a compact fern with hanging fronds and wavy leaflets; "Teddy Junior", which has wrinkled, wavy leaves. Multi-pinnate cultivated varieties include "Bornstedt" with very delicate leaves and rounded tips; "Rooseveltii Plumosa" which has bipinnate leaves and deeply indented or pinnate, frizzy leaflets; "Whitemanii" which has broad, hanging, multi-parted fronds and deeply indented or pinnate leaflets.

Nephrolepis cordifolia,
Curly fern
Nephrolepis exaltata,
Curly fern

Onoclea sensibilis

Onoclea

☐ ⊘ ↕ 30-60

Onoclea is indigenous in North America and North East Asia. It owes its name to the large number of small, brown bulbs with sori on the fertile leaves. The infertile fronds have a clearly distinct shape. *O. sensibilis*, the sole species in this genus, grows only in moist, marshy areas.

This is a spreading fern which is suitable for ground cover in a large garden, by a pond in shady spots. It requires moist, slightly acid soil, rich in humus, e.g., a mixture of loam, leaf-mould or peat and sharp sand. If it is sufficiently moist, the fern can also survive in full sunlight. Propagate by dividing the plant.

O. sensibilis has creeping rootstocks which grow underground, branching out and expanding rapidly. In spring the reddish infertile leaves develop at some distance from each other (they are susceptible to night frost). They develop into pale-green, large, triangular pinnate leaves with long stems with pairs of broad, indented or serrated leaflets. In the autumn they turn from yellow to brown and are then shed. The smaller, narrower, erect, fertile leaves develop in summer; they are rather like plumes because of the numerous brown capsules of spores. They are not shed in winter and are therefore suitable for bouquets of dried flowers; the capsules burst open the following spring.

*Onoclea sensibilis
and Meconopsis cambrica*

45

Osmunda regalis, Royal fern

Osmunda
Royal fern

○ ⊘ ⬆ 100-200 ✳

Osmunda is a cosmopolitan genus which is found everywhere except in Australia. It includes some very striking ferns. *O. regalis*, which is also found in our part of the world by ditches and in moist woodlands and in peaty soil, is a protected species in a number of European countries (including the Netherlands) and may not be removed from its natural habitat. The finely chopped roots of these ferns are used as a growth medium (potting compost) for orchids and other epiphytic plants.

The rootstock of this fern protrudes above the ground several centimetres like a short trunk covered with leaf sheaths and roots, and a crown of large, strong, pinnate or bipinnate leaves which can grow to a length of 2-3 m. The fertile and infertile fronds are clearly distinct. In some fertile fronds the upper leaves may be entirely covered with ripe brown sori so that they can look rather wilted at the top. Cultivars do not grow to the same height as ferns in the wild.

This is an excellent fern to grow in sunny, very moist, or shady slightly drier spots, on its own as a border plant. It requires moist acid soil rich in humus, e.g., a mixture of loam, sharp sand and leaf-mould or peat. Do not remove dead fronds as they provide cover in winter. They can be removed later. Propagate by dividing clumps in spring or sowing the fresh spores directly into moist potting compost in summer.

O. cinnamomea, the cinnamon fern, has groups of erect, fertile fronds, 50-150 cm long, which develop in spring with small leaflets like slender plumes with cinnamon-coloured sori. They turn from green to brown and are shed after dispersing the spores. The pinnate, infertile leaves, which are just as tall and curve at the top,

Osmunda regalis,
Royal fern

47

Osmunda claytoniana,
Royal fern
and Hydrocotyle
Novae-Zelandiae

develop slightly later with narrow, lanceolate, lobed leaves which remain green in summer. It cannot tolerate dry conditions (the edges of the leaves turn brown).
O. claytoniana has pinnate leaves, 100-120 cm long, with a number of small fertile leaflets in the middle covered with sori which dry up when the spores have been dispersed; the other leaflets are long and lobed and stay green until the fronds die off; beautiful yellow autumn colours.
O. regalis has sturdy, bipinnate, infertile leaves, 50-180 cm long, with long blunt leaflets on the outside; the fertile, slightly longer fronds develop within these with a sort of plume at the top consisting of narrow leaflets which turn from green to

brown because of the sori; in colder regions the fern loses its leaves. *O. regalis* "Cristata" has frizzy leaves; "Purpurascens", the purple royal fern, has deep pink stems in spring which turn purple later, dark green fronds and golden brown, fertile leaves which bear the spores.

Osmunda regalis
"Purpurascens",
Purple royal fern

Pellaea

⊘ ⊚ ↕ 30-50 🪣 ✄

Pellaea originally comes mainly from dry, rather rocky regions in North and South America, Africa, Asia and New Zealand. It is a low to medium spreading fern with brittle, rigid, dark stems, and leathery, pinnate or multipinnate, dark green leaves. The sori are always along the edges of the leaves.

A number of species are very suitable as indoor plants, although a few winter-hardy species can also be grown in a rockery, such as *P. atropurpurea*, which has rigid, hairy, purplish-black stems, triangular leaves 25-30 cm long, parted many times at the base, and widespread, lanceolate leaflets which turn from green to a bluish-green. Grow in a shady, well-drained spot, in lime-rich soil. It is only evergreen when the winters are mild. Protect against heavy rain. Indoors the fern thrives in broad, shallow dishes or (hanging) baskets because of its shallow roots, even in fairly dark spots. It requires light, well-drained soil, rich in humus, e.g., equal parts of sand or vermiculite, leaf-mould or peat, and some lime. Keep relatively moist and do not allow the plant to dry out. Do not water the leaves directly - especially in winter - to

Pellaea aff. falcata

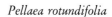
Pellaea rotundifolia

Pellaea rotundifolia

prevent infections, and spray occasionally. Temperature 14-20° C, in winter 12-15° C. During the growing season, feed once every two or three weeks. Propagate by dividing in spring.

P. falcata, has a creeping rootstock, short, rather hairy stems, lanceolate, dark green pinnate leaves, 20-30 cm long, with closely packed, sickle-shaped leaflets.

P. rotundifolia has thin, brown, hairy stems, and shiny, dark greenish-bronze pinnate leaves, 15-30 cm long, with numerous round to oval leaflets.

P. viridis (syn. *P. hastata*) has shiny stems, triangular, light green bipinnate leaves, 30-50 cm long, and long, oval leaflets.

Phlebodium

⊘ ◉ ↕ 100-120 🏺 ✂

Phlebodium is indigenous in tropical South America and was first cultivated in England in 1740. There is some disagreement whether the approximately 10 different species are varieties of *P. aureum*, the only species which is cultivated.

This fern is an epiphytic plant which grows on trees, with thick, scaly, creeping rootstocks and large, broad, deeply indented fronds with long stems.

This is an excellent, strong indoor fern for light or rather dark spots. Protect it from sunlight; it is fairly resistant to dry conditions. It requires porous, slightly acid soil, rich in humus, e.g., a mixture of sharp sand, leaf-mould and some bonemeal. Always keep moderately moist, spray occasionally with (rain)water which does not contain much lime. Temperature 18-22° C, in winter 10-16° C. Feed once or twice a month during the growing season (half concentration). Repot in spring.

Propagate by dividing rootstocks and from spores.

P. aureum has long, creeping light golden-brown, scaly rootstocks which grow over the edge of the plant pot, fairly long, yellowish stems (approximately 50 cm), and broad, bluish, four-lobed leaves, 50-60 cm long, 30-60 cm wide, with long, undulating leaflets tapering to a point. The striking orange sori are distributed regularly over the undersides of the leaves. *P. aureum* "Cristatum" has frizzy leaflets; "Mandaianum" has regularly indented, undulating, frizzy leaflets.

Phlebodium aureum

Phyllitis
Hart's tongue

◉ ↕ 20-60 ✳ 🏺

Phyllitis is indigenous in temperate and subtropical regions of the northern hemisphere, and is fairly common in humid, lime-rich areas; in this part of the world it is less common, but is found in rocky woodlands, on damp walls, in wells and in dunes.

This evergreen fern has a short, sturdy rootstock, short, hairy, scaly stems, shiny, leathery, unparted, slightly wavy, tongue-shaped leaves in groups, which are heart-shaped at the base, and taper to a point with long, narrow sori.

This fern grows in moist, shady spots in woodland gardens (under early flowering shrubs), in rockeries and on walls. It requires loose, porous soil, e.g., a mixture of loam, sharp sand, extra leaf-mould or peat, and some lime. Always keep moist but not too wet. Protect from the sun in winter. Indoors it is suitable in darker places (north-facing window), the soil should

Phyllitis scolopendrium "Ramosa Cristata", Hart's tongue

Phyllitis scolopendrium, Hart's tongue

always be moist but not too wet, consisting of, e.g., potting compost, leaf-mould or peat, sharp sand, some bonemeal and lime. It can be placed on an upturned saucer in a dish of water. It requires plenty of fresh air, temperature during the day, 18-24° C, at night 7-13° C; feed in spring and summer (half concentration). Repot annually in spring. Propagate by sowing spores - plants grown from cultivars often look different from the parent plants. They can also be propagated from cuttings.

P. scolopendrium (syn. *Scolopendrium vulgare, Asplenium scolopendrium*) has erect, shiny green leaves, 20-45 cm long, and 3-6 cm wide. There are many cultivars with different shaped leaves: hanging, forked,

extremely wavy, crested, deeply indented, etc. *P. scolopendrium* "Crispum" has pleated leaves; "Crispum Nobile" has dark green leaves, 60 cm long and 12 cm wide; "Cristatum" has curling or wavy leaves; "Undulata" has very wavy leaves, 10-15 cm long.

54

Phyllitis scolopendrium
"Crispa", Hart's tongue

Pilularia
Pillwort

⊘ ↕ 4-14 ✳

The name *Pilularia* comes from the Latin
word "pilula" (pill), and the English name
pillwort refers to the capsules of spores
which are like hard, round pills at the base
of the leaf sheaths. The six species are
indigenous in marshy areas in Europe,
North America, Australia and New Zealand;
P. globulifera also grows in this country in
drier places, and in shallow waters lacking
in nutrients.
This is a grassy fern with a wiry rootstock,

creeping stems and cylindrical, wiry leaves.
This is a small fern, suitable for shady spots,
by the water's edge, in a (shallow) pond, or
in an aquarium on peaty soil, covered with
water. Propagate by dividing plant.
P. globulifera has long, creeping stems, thin,
erect, light green leaves, 3-14 cm long. The
young leaves are coiled in spirals, the spores
are contained in brownish-black, hairy
capsules.
P. minuta is a lower fern, with densely
packed leaves, 5-6 cm long.

Pilularia globulifera,
Pillwort

56

Platycerium
Hart's-horn fern

  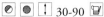 30-90

Platycerium is indigenous in the tropical jungles of South America, Australia, Africa and Asia, where it grows on trees as an epiphytic plant. In its natural habitat the leaves can grow up to 5 m long. Its popularity as an indoor plant has fluctuated. This fern has clearly distinguishable fertile and infertile leaves: the erect, shell-shaped, overlapping infertile leaves turn from green to brown and dry out, arranged like overlapping scales to protect the stems and roots, while humus is formed underneath from rotting matter; in the middle there are long, hanging or erect, forked antler-like fertile leaves with hard, brown, powdery capsules of spores on the underside. A layer of wax protects the leaves against excessive evaporation. The plant tolerates dry conditions well and is particularly suitable for centrally heated rooms.

The fern comes into its own best in shady or very dark spots, hanging on the wall, tied to a tree trunk, or in a hanging basket, with a mixture of peat, moss and beech leaves or loose peat. Do not water too often; in hot weather, immerse once a week, when the weather is cooler, once a fortnight. Add feed to the water during the growing season in spring and summer (half concentration).

Platycerium bifurcatum
ssp. bifurcatum
var. bifurcatum,
Hart's-horn fern

Platycerium bifurcatum
ssp. bifurcatum
var. hillii,
Hart's-horn fern

Temperature 20° C., slightly lower in
winter. Do not dust the leaves or remove
the brown points (so that spores can form),
and do not spray. Propagate by removing
runners and sowing spores.
B. bifurcatum has rounded, infertile leaves,
up to 30 cm long, which turn brown
quickly and are not very indented, and
light, greyish-green, bifurcated or trifurcated
fertile leaves, coated with white felt, up to
90 cm long; the lower half of these is
covered with brown spore capsules. It has a
number of subspecies and varieties, such as
P. bifurcatum ssp. *willinckii* (syn.
P. willinckii) with fairly large, uneven forked
bracts, and creeping, deeply indented, white,
hairy, fertile leaves. *P. bifurcatum* ssp.
bifurcatum var. *hillii* (syn. *P. hilli*) has
kidney-shaped infertile leaves and erect,
fertile leaves which fan out; *B. bifurcatum*
"San Diego" has shiny, dark green leaves
and broader round leaflets.
P. grande has nest-shaped, erect, low,
infertile leaves, 30 cm long, and hanging,
branched, antler-like fertile leaves,
30-200 cm long, with slightly hairy, broad,
lanceolate leaflets, and sori at the first
branches.

58

Platycerium coronarium,
Hart's-horn fern

Polypodium vulgare,
Polypody

Polypodium
Polypody

⊘ ↕ 15-60 ❋

Polypodium is found throughout the world and comprises numerous species. *P. vulgare,* which is common throughout Europe, is found in shady spots, in dunes and woodlands, on tree trunks, pollarded willows and old walls - it is also suitable for rockeries. Some tropical species can also be cultivated indoors in hanging baskets if treated with care.

This fern has creeping, branched rootstocks, leathery leaves which leave a scar when they drop off; the large, round uncovered sori are arranged in one or two lines on the back of the leaflets.

This is an evergreen fern for shady spots in rocky or woodland gardens. It can be grown on its own in fairly poor, stony soil, rich in humus, e.g., a mixture of peat or leaf-mould, sharp sand, vermiculite, and some bonemeal. Keep fairly moist, but not too wet, and feed in spring and summer (half concentration). Propagate by dividing the rootstock.

P. interjectum, intermediate polypody, has slightly triangular, four-lobed leaves, 15-50 cm long, pointed, serrated leaflets, the lowest pair of which is set forward, and oval sori; it forms new leaves from May to June, and sheds the old leaves. *P. interjectum* "Cornubiense" has beautiful, pale green, pinnate leaves. If necessary, give extra water in summer.

P. vulgare, common polypody, has thick, scaly rootstocks with a sweet taste, four-lobed leaves, 8-40 cm long, with blunt, slightly curved leaflets, which are not serrated, and round sori. There are various cultivars with curled and frizzy leaflets, such as *P. vulgare* "Bifido Multifidum", with finely parted, crested leaflets.

Because of the superficial system of roots, it is best to cultivate the ferns indoors in shallow pots or hanging baskets, in light spots protected from sunlight. It requires well-drained, moist soil, not too wet, e.g., a mixture of peat or leaf-mould and vermiculite. Spray regularly, temperature during the day 21-25° C, at night 10-15° C. Feed once a month during the growing season (half concentration). Propagate by dividing rootstocks.

↕ 40- 200 ▣ ◁

P. crassifolium has tongue-shaped leaves, 30-90 cm long, with a smooth, wavy edge. *P. subauriculatum* (syn. *Goniophlebium subauriculatum*) has short, creeping, dark brown, scaly rootstocks, shiny dark stems, 20-30 cm long, hanging pinnate leaves, 100-200 cm long and 30-40 cm wide, with numerous long, serrated leaflets and round sori. *P. subauriculatum* "Knightise" has large fronds with frizzy leaflets.

Polypodium vulgare,
Polypody

Polypodium vulgare,
Polypody

Polystichum
Shield fern

⬤ ⊘ ↕ 30-100 ✳ ⬚ ✦

Polystichum is a very common genus found in many places, particularly in temperate regions and tropical mountain areas. A few species, such as *P. aculeatum*, the hard shield fern, and *P. setiferum*, the soft shield fern, are indigenous in our own country and grow in shady places in woodlands, on banks and old walls.

This is a sturdy, bushy fern with scaly stems and beautiful, often leathery, dark green, symmetrical, long, pointed fronds, which can be pinnate or bipinnate. The edges of the leaflets often have sharp teeth tapering to a sharp point.

A number of evergreen species are suitable for (semi) shady spots in the garden. They require fertile soil which is always moist, but not too wet, e.g., a mixture of loam, sharp sand, leaf-mould or peat, and some lime. Cover in winter if necessary.

Propagate by dividing the clumps in spring.

P. acrostichoides, Christmas fern, has creeping rootstocks and shiny, dark green pinnate leaves, 30-90 cm long, with ear-shaped, lobed leaflets at the base. The infertile leaves are evergreen. It requires soil rich in lime and humus, and preferably stony ground. Suitable for use as greenery.

P. aculeatum, the hard shield fern, has erect, shiny, dark green, lanceolate bipinnate leaves with serrated leaflets. The old leaves are shed when the new leaves develop. It is very sensitive to dry conditions, and is extremely suitable for an evergreen garden, e.g., by water.

P. lonchitis, the holly fern, has very narrow, stiff pinnate leaves, 20-60 cm long, in compact groups. Suitable for humid rockeries. Protect against winter sunlight.

P. makinoi has orangey-brown fronds in spring, 50 cm long.

P. munitum is less hardy in winter. It has pinnate leaves, 50-100 cm long, with sword-shaped leaflets close together, with spiny edges. It is very sensitive to dry conditions. Cover in winter if necessary. It can be grown amongst ground cover.

P. setiferum, the soft shield fern, has elegantly curving, soft, pale matt green, bipinnate leaves, 30-100 cm long, suitable for very shady spots. There are many cultivars which are more or less evergreen, e.g., *P. setiferum* "Herrenhausen", which forms extremely large clumps and has beautiful broad fronds, 70 cm long;

Polystichum setiferum,
Shield fern

*Polystichum setiferum
"Divisilobum Densum",
Shield fern*

*Polystichum setiferum
"Congestum",
Shield fern*

"Proliferum Plumosum Densum" is a plumy fern with scaly, finely divided leaves and overlapping leaflets. In winter it has rust-brown as well as dark green leaves. Suitable for growing on its own in smaller gardens.

P. tsus-sinense has very dark green, bipinnate leaves, 15-30 cm long, which taper to a point, and leaflets which end in sharp points. It comes from regions with heavy snowfall and should be covered in winter. Do not place in direct sunlight.

The dwarf variety, *P. tsus-sinense*, is also available as an indoor fern for cool, light spots, protected from the sun. It requires nutritious, moist soil, not too wet, e.g., a mixture of potting compost, leaf-mould, sharp sand and some bonemeal. Temperature 7-18° C. Always keep moderately moist, preferably with rainwater, and spray regularly. It can be placed on an upturned saucer in a dish of water. Feed in spring and summer (half concentration). Repot in spring. Propagate by dividing clumps (in spring) and by sowing spores.

Pteridium

Bracken

◎ ↕ 60-300 ✳

There is only one species of *Pteridium*,
P. aquilinium, which is a truly cosmopolitan
fern. It is found throughout the world in
temperate, tropical and subtropical regions,
in woodlands and on open (cleared) ground,
in acid, sandy and loamy soil, poor in
nutrients. When the stem is cut diagonally,
the dark coloured veins reveal a "double
eagle", which explains the Latin name of
the plant. It is poisonous to domestic
animals and is avoided by rabbits etc.
This is a strong, spreading fern which can
be used as ground cover for parks and
woodland gardens in poor soil. It grows in
light, shady spots in moist or light, dry soil,
poor in lime, e.g., a mixture of loam, sharp
sand, leaf-mould or peat. Propagate by

dividing rootstocks (in spring) and sowing
spores.
P. aquilinium, bracken, has black, thick,
long, hairy rootstocks which creep
underground, from which tough,
brownish-green stems, 30-90 cm tall, grow
up at irregular distances. First these have
young, greyish-white hairy leaves; later they
are leathery, triangular, bipinnate to
quadripinnate leaves which are 30-60 cm
long, and can even grow to 3 m in
favourable conditions. They have long, blunt
or pointed leaflets and sori in thin lines
along and underneath the curled edges of
the leaflets. There are also varieties with
frizzy or crested fronds. In the autumn the
leaves turn a golden yellow before dying
off; they develop again in spring.

Pteridium aquilinium,
Bracken

Pteris

⊘ ◉ ↕ 25-100 ⊔ ⊠

Pteris is mainly indigenous in tropical and subtropical regions, and to a lesser extent in temperate zones. It grows in moist woodlands. The lower two leaflets of the fronds look like butterfly wings. This fern has a short, scaly, often creeping rootstock and green or variegated, usually pinnate leaves with long stems, which can have lobed, serrated, frizzy, crested or wrinkled leaflets. The edges of the fertile leaflets curl around the sori on the underside.

This is a decorative indoor fern for light, shady spots, out of the sunlight. Variegated plants require a lighter spot. It requires soil rich in humus, but with not too much lime, e.g., a mixture of potting compost, sharp sand, peat (or beech), leaf-mould and some bonemeal. Always keep moist. It needs a high humidity level, so spray frequently, preferably with rainwater (poor in lime). Temperature, 21-26° C, cooler in winter (10-12° C). Variegated varieties, at least 16-18° C. All the ferns are sensitive to salt. Feed twice a month during the growing season (half concentration). Remove older, ugly fronds. Repot in spring if necessary, and remove old earth. Propagate by dividing clumps and sowing spores. Sensitive to scale insects.

P. cretica has yellow or light green erect stems, 10-30 cm long, and leathery, pale green pinnate leaves, 20-30 cm long, and 15-20 cm wide, with lanceolate or ribbon-shaped, serrated or indented leaflets. This fern is less sensitive to dry conditions. There are many cultivars with green or variegated fronds with different shapes, e.g., *P. cretica* "Albolineata" with broader fronds, has leaflets forming a white stripe along its length in the middle; "Mayi" has narrower leaflets with a greyish-green stripe in the middle and crested branching ends. "Parkeri" has broad, green serrated fronds; "Roeweri" has long, narrow fronds with stems, and long leaflets with a frizzy crest at the top; "Wilsonii" has compact, fan-shaped, bright green fronds with tufted ends; "Wimsettii" has broad, deeply indented, pointed, irregularly parted, frizzy fronds.

P. ensiformis has thin yellow stems, pinnate leaves which are bipinnate at the base, spreading, blunt, infertile fronds, 20-45 cm long, with elliptical, extremely serrated leaflets and longer, erect, fertile fronds with wavy, smooth-edged leaflets and a long terminal leaflet. *P. ensiformis* "Evergemiensis" has white variegated fronds. *P. faurei* has dark green pinnate leaves with

top: Pteris cretica
bottom: Pteris cretica "Albolineata"

top: Pteris ensiformis "Evergemiensis"
bottom: Pteris faurei

slightly wavy edges. It tolerates drier air.
P. multifida (syn. *P. serrulata*) has brown
stems, narrow, dark green pinnate leaves,
30-60 cm long, which are far apart and are
bipinnate at the base. They have long, very
narrow leaflets; *P. multifida* "Cristata" has
frizzy leaflets with crested ends.
P. quadriaurita has straw-coloured stems,
and triangular, bipinnate or tripinnate
leaves, 50 cm long; *P. quadriaurita*
"Argyreia" has a greenish-white line down
the middle; "Tricolor" has a silvery-white
line down the middle.
P. tremula grows quickly and fully at the
base, but is more spread out later on. It has
brown stems, 5-30 cm long, pale green
multipinnate leaves up to 100 cm long, and
coarse, strikingly lobed, overlapping leaflets.
It does not tolerate dry air. In summer it
can be placed outside, out of the sunlight
and dug into the ground.

Pteris quadriaurita "Tricolor"

Salvinia

○ ↕ 2-2,5

Salvinia is indigenous in tropical areas throughout the world, in stagnant and sluggish water. In warm weather it can proliferate and cover a large surface area. This is an attractive floating fern which has groups of three leaves quite far apart, on thin, branching stems. There are two oval leaflets floating on the water and one hanging into the water, divided into hair-shaped leaflets which resemble roots, with spherical sori.
This water fern is not winter-hardy, and is suitable for shallow ponds or indoors for a terrarium or aquarium. It requires a light, shady spot, but can be placed in a protected position in the sun in summer. It grows in freshwater: water temperature, 18-25° C, and requires soil rich in humus, e.g., equal parts of potting compost, sharp sand, peat or leaf-mould. Propagate by dividing at any time.
S. auriculata (also available under the name *S. natans*) has broad, oval, bright green, slightly spreading leaves, 2-2.5 cm long, which lie flat on the water. In strong light they grow larger and may be so close together that the edges of the leaves protrude above the surface of the water. The undersides are covered with brown hairs.
S. rotundifolia has round leaves 2 cm long. The tops of the leaves are covered with stiff hairs.

Salvinia natans

Thelypteris
Marsh fern

◯ ◐ ↕ 30-100 ✳

Thelypteris is found almost all over the world in temperate and subtropical regions. A number of species, such as *T. palustris* (marsh fern), *T. oreopteris* (mountain fern) and *T. phegopteris* (beech fern) are indigenous in this country. The former are found in fens and marshes; the two others in moist, deciduous woodland.

This fern has thin, creeping, often scaly, hairy rootstocks, broad, usually pinnate leaves with deeply indented leaflets and round sori on the lower sides and the side veins.

It sheds its leaves and is suitable for sunny or light, shady spots. It requires moist or very moist soil, rich in humus. Propagate by dividing rootstocks (spring) and sowing spores.

T. hexagonoptera (syn. *Dryopteris hexagonoptera, Phegopteris hexagonoptera*), broad beech fern, has branching, creeping rootstocks from which the broad, lanceolate

Thelypteris phegopteris,
Beech fern

Thelypteris palustris,
Marsh fern

fronds, 25-30 cm long, arise close together. These have light to dark green, deeply indented, wavy leaflets. It requires a sheltered spot.

T. noveboracensis (syn. *Aspidium noveboracensis, Dryopteris noveboracensis*) has pale green, deeply indented fronds, 30-60 cm long, and rounded leaflets. In a moist spot it can tolerate sunlight.

T. oreopteris (syn. *Dryopteris oreopteris, Oreopteris limbosperma*) (mountain fern) has bright, yellowish-green, lanceolate fronds and long or lanceolate leaflets covered with yellow glands at the bottom. The sori are near to the edges of the leaves. When the leaves are rubbed, they have a strong lemony scent. This fern grows in acid, moist, sandy soil, rich in humus.

T. palustris (syn. *Aspidium thelypteris, Dryopteris thelypteris*) (marsh fern) has long, thin, black rootstocks with long stems arising from them at some distance from each other, with bright green, lanceolate, deeply indented, infertile fronds, 15-80 cm long, which have smooth leaflets and longer, slender fertile fronds (up to 100 cm) with thicker leaflets and sori under the turned-over edges of the leaves. Suitable for shady, lime-free spots, e.g., by a pond.

T. phegopteris (syn. *Dryopteris phegopteris, Phegopteris connectilis, Polypodium phegopteris*) (beech fern) has long, brittle stems, 10-45 cm tall, triangular, bipinnate, olive green leaves, and deeply indented leaflets. The lowest pair is furthest away from the others and bends downwards. This fern grows in shady, lime-free spots, and is suitable for ground cover, under shrubs or small trees.

Thelypteris phegopteris, Beech fern

69

Woodsia polystichoides

Woodsia

⊘ ↕ 5-40 ✳

Woodsia is indigenous in rocky areas in northern Europe, North America and northern Asia. It grows in the poorest soil and is very suitable for rockeries.

This is a delicate fern with a short, scaly rootstock, narrow, erect, long, bipinnate fronds which grow in groups, and round sori along the edges of the leaflets on the back of the fertile fronds.

This fern sheds its leaves and grows in the rockery in a light, shady spot between the stones or against the wall, in moist, rather wet soil, e.g., a mixture of loam, sharp sand, leaf-mould or peat. (*W. obtusa* needs some ground lime.) Propagate by dividing rootstocks (spring) or sowing spores.

W. alpina, has narrow fronds, 5-15 cm long, and slightly scaly, triangular leaflets.

W. ilvensis has reddish-brown, hairy stems and lacy fronds, 7-20 cm long and 3 cm wide, with a smooth upper side and a scaly, brown, hairy underside. It requires an acid, rather damp spot.

W. obtusa has greyish fronds, 15-40 cm long, with white hair on both sides and rounded leaflets. It is evergreen or semi-evergreen and tolerates calcareous soil.

W. scopulina has fronds which are 15-20 cm long, with deeply indented leaflets.

70

Woodwardia

○ ⊘ ◉ ↕ 40-200 ✳

Woodwardia is indigenous in marshy areas, in southern Europe, North America and Asia.

This is a large fern with long, forked, sturdy rootstocks which grow rapidly. It has deeply indented, hanging fronds and a double row of spores on the back of the fertile leaves.

This fern sheds its leaves and requires a great deal of space in the sun, in light shade, or in a fairly dark spot. It grows in marshy, acid soil, e.g., a mixture of loam, sharp sand, leaf-mould or peat. If necessary, water with lime-free water. Propagate by dividing rootstocks (in spring), or from spores. *W. radicans* can be propagated fairly easily by removing young plants which take root in good potting compost.

W. areolata (syn. *W. angustifolia*) has long, slender, green stems. The infertile fronds are 40-60 cm long, with broad, wavy leaflets tapering to a point, which change from red to a shiny green. The long, fertile fronds develop in the autumn with smooth, very narrow leaflets.

W. fimriata (syn. *W. chamissoi*) has large fronds which grow up to 250 cm long and 40 cm broad in their natural habitat (U.S.). The cultivars are not as tall.

W. radicans has fronds which are up to 200 cm long and 50 cm wide, with oval to lanceolate, lobed leaflets. The young plants develop at the ends of the fronds. This fern is not winter-hardy.

W. virginica is a creeping fern with lanceolate fronds, 60-120 cm long, and coarsely serrated leaflets, which turn from a yellowish-green to a dark green.

Woodwardia radicans

Survey of garden and indoor ferns; please refer to the descriptions for specific varieties and data.

GARDEN FERNS

Sun - partial shade	height in cm	hardy	ever-green	Partial shade - shade	height in cm	hardy	ever-green
Ceterach	-20	*	*	Adiantum	15-50	half	*
Cystopteris	10-60	*		Asplenium	5-45	*	*
Dennstaedtia	30-200	*		Athyrium	-80	*	*
Matteuccia	-150	*	*	Blechnum	15-65	half	*
Onoclea	30-60	*	*	Cheilanthes	-30	half	*
Osmunda	100-200	*		Dryopteris	30-150	*	semi
Salvinia	2-2,5			Gymnocarpium	10-45	*	
Thelypteris	30-100	*		Pellaea	30-50	*	semi
Woodwardia	40-200	half		Phyllitis	20-60	*	*
				Pilularia	4-14	*	
				Polypodium	15-60	*	*
				Polystichum	30-100	*	*
				Pteridium	60-300	*	
				Woodsia	5-40	*.	

Groundcover:
Blechnum
Dennstaedtia
Onoclea
Pteridium
Thelypteris

Border:
Asplenium
Athyrium
Dennstaedtia
Gymnocarpium
Osmunda
Pellaea
Thelypteris

Woodland fern:
Dryopteris
Matteuccia
Phyllitis
Polypodium
Pteridium
Thelypteris

Marginals/Pond Plants:
Athyrium
Matteuccia
Onoclea
Pilularia
Salvinia
Thelypteris

Rock garden:
Asplenium
Blechnum
Ceterach
Cheilanthes
Cystopteris
Gymnocarpium
Pellaea
Phyllitis
Polypodium
Polystichum
Woodsia

Single:
Matteuccia
Osmunda
Polypodium
Polystichum
Woodwardia

INDOOR FERNS
Partial shade - shade, protect against sun

	height in cm	keep moist	spray	temp in °C day	night	winter
Adiantum	30-75	semi	*	18		
Asplenium	60-100	semi	*	18-22	16	12
Blechnum	-100	constant	*	16-24		14
Cibotium	100-200	semi		21-26	10-15	
Cyathea	200-300	constant	*(stem)	21-26	18	
Cyrtomium	30-40	semi	*	16-20	10-12	7-10
Davallia	30-85	semi	*	20-24	7-15	
Dicksonia	100-200	constant	*(stem)	21-26	18	
Didymochlaena	150-200	constant	*	20-22		
Doryopteris	30-70	semi		24-26	15-21	
Humata	20-30	semi		21-26	10-15	
Microlepia	30-50	semi	*	18-22		15
Nephrolepis	30-70	semi	*	18-22		18
Pellaea	30-50	semi	*	14-20		12-15
Phlebodium	100-120	semi	*	18-22		10-16
Phyllitis	20-60	semi		18-24	7-13	
Platycerium	30-90	semi		20		12-15
Polypodium	40-200	semi	*	21-26	10-15	
Polystichum	30-100	semi	*	7-18		
Pteris	25-100	semi	*	21-26		10-12

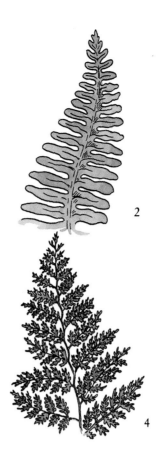

Leaf Shapes
1. Undivided or
non-laciniate leaf
(eg. Tongue fern)
2. Deep laciniate to
single pinnate leaf
(Sword fern)
3. Double pinnate leaf
(Athyrium filix-femina).
4. Double composite
of triple pinnate leaf
(Davillia).

The remarkable sex life of ferns

1. Formation of spores in the capsule (sporangia) underneath a fertile leaf.
2. When they are ripe, the millions of spores are thrown out by the sporangia when it bursts open.
3. A spore that lands on good soil (moist and light) produces a prothallium (of approx. 6 mm), onto which male and female organs develop. The spermatozoa from the male organ swim across moisture to fertilise the eggs.
4. On the prothalium the impregnated egg creates a new plant which takes root; the first leaves have an aberrant shape.

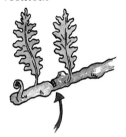

1. Force the rootstock to divide by making an incision at the end just before a bulge (bud) to half its size.

2. After 8 or 9 weeks, cut off entirely (after root shaped section, which must be at least 5 cm long); dig out carefully with sufficient soil.

3. Plant promptly in desired spot at original depth. Water well, push down the soil.

Planting and Maintenance

Ferns are decorative foliage plants, which often prefer moisture and a high atmospheric humidity, but do not like bright sun and wind or draughts. They usually prefer a moist soil rich in humus, and cool, partially shaded habitats. In spring, the young leaves unfurl in a characteristic manner, generally differing in colour from the fully-grown leaf. In the autumn they can display the most beautiful autumn colours. The leaves of many varieties are suitable for picking and in flower arrangements; dried fern leaf is also very attractive.

Ferns propagate by means of spores. Sometimes these are formed on special, fertile leaves which look different from the 'usual' sterile leaf and are referred to as Hard Fern.

In the garden

Both in a formal and in a more natural planting scheme, many varieties are suitable for planting underneath shrubs and trees. Some varieties make excellent ground covers, several are suitable for rock gardens and walls, others look attractive as pond marginals or solitary border plants. During the winter a number of evergreens will define the appearance of the garden. Ferns can also be successfully cultivated in pots on the balcony or patio, even when these are north facing.

In order to make a sufficiently humus-rich soil, leaf mould or peat dust can be added. In the autumn fallen leaves from trees and shrubs make a good supplement: the cover prevents evaporation, limits the growth of weeds and becomes humus again after decomposition. Fertilising is usually not necessary; on poor soil a little lime (bone meal or fish meal) can have a positive effect. The plants should be watered regularly during dry weather in the summer.

Varieties with creeping rootstocks should be planted near the surface, the others always as deeply as where they were planted before; the soil should always be pressed down lightly and evenly.

Small differences in height can be created with peat bricks, which soak up and retain the moisture well. The paths should be sprinkled with bark or mulch.

New plants are produced by separating the clump, dividing the rootstock or sowing the spores. The latter is not always that easy, although it sometimes happens naturally.

When using a planting scheme which incorporates trees, deep-rooting varieties with a light crown, such as birch, are preferable. Other plants which can be combined successfully with ferns are: all kinds of bulbous plants - eg. Wood anemones, Snowdrops and Lilies - and woodland plants - Wood violets, Aquilegias, Foxgloves, Christmas roses, Lungwort and Rhododendrons (on acid soil). Periwinkle (Vinca) and Ivy provide very good ground cover.

	Spring	Autumn	Winter
Planting	**	*	
Cutting away leaf	**		
Sowing/dividing	**	*	
Covering		*	*

* = possibly; ** = preferably.

In the home

Ferns for growing indoors are generally very demanding in terms of atmospheric humidity and temperature. The light requirement is different for each variety. Ferns with a leathery leaf lose less moisture through evaporation and are therefore especially suited to indoor conditions.

The pot clump must be kept evenly moist, but not too wet. Always use plastic pots with a good layer of crocks at the bottom, or use special pots with a built-in watering system. Occasionally you can sink the pot in water.

Ferns will not always last very long indoors, although when well looked after, repotted on time and watered regularly, they can retain their beauty for years. As they are sturdy growers, it may be necessary to repot them several times a year; make sure that the old clump remains intact. Sometimes good results can be achieved during a resting period, when the plant is watered less, put in a cool position and the old leaf removed. Repot the plant after six weeks and try to establish new growth.

Ferns are not very susceptible to disease and pests, but when they are neglected, greenfly, woolly aphid, scale insect or thrips can attack. When that happens, there is no other option but to put the plant outside for a while, weather permitting; or to throw it out.
Other good places to grow ferns are greenhouses, conservatories or glass frames.

	Spring	*Growing season*	*Autumn/winter*
Repotting	**		if necessary
Fertilising		1-2 x per month	1x per month
Dividing	**		
Rest	-------------------------if necessary-------------------------		

* = possibly; ** = preferably.

Buying tips

Ferns in the wild should be left undisturbed, even though there are varieties which can be propagated simply and without damage from a single runner or rootstock.
It is best to find a reliable supplier who has a wide choice and can answer questions.
For the advanced gardener there are specialised nurseries and, occasionally, garden centres.
Common ferns, readily available, are as follows (under the trade name a whole genus usually lies hidden):
Adiantum (Maidenhair) - there are hundreds of varieties;
Asplenium (including Hen-and-chicken fern);
Nephrolepis exaltata (Sword Fern), the most widely-sold fern by far;
Pelleae (including Button-fern), of which a number of varieties are hardy;
Platycerium (Stag's-horn fern, usually the common *P. bifurcatum*) and *Pteris* (including the Spider fern and Snow brake), a plant that is easy to grow.
In general, the following rules apply: buy ferns the way you would buy fruit and vegetables - the ones that make your mouth water.
Leaves which are too pale, brown and mold can be signs of disease or bad conditions.
Ferns are not particularly prone to disease and they can be cultivated in an environmentally friendly way. The ferns in a mixed tray pictured above/below are in optimum condition.

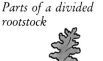

Parts of a divided rootstock

1. Cut off stock (c. 5 cm long) with leaf and dig out.

2. Plant as deeply as before, support the leaf, remove top half (do not give too much food and water).

Ferns mixed

Small workers in the garden

Blackbird, *Turdus merula*
Earthworm,
Lumbricus terrestris
Hedgehog, *Erinaceus europaeus*

Life round the ferns
Most ferns are shade-loving plants. Their greenery adorns the shady areas underneath trees and shrubs. In general, they flourish in fairly moist soil. Beneath the surface these places are the domain of very different inhabitants: earthworms.

Slug,
Arion ater

Earthworms

Earthworms are very useful creatures. While they are eating, they enrich the soil. They literally eat their way through the earth, and the organic material in the soil which they do not digest is excreted above the ground or just below the surface. These products of excretion are mixed in the worm's body - which consists of no fewer than 150 segments - with lime and other useful matter. In this way valuable minerals and other essential natural components which had drained down to deeper levels of the soil in rainwater, are brought up again to provide nutrients for plant roots. By their steady digging they also ensure that the soil is broken down and crumbly so that air and water can penetrate easily. All in all, we cannot do without worms in the garden, and the garden certainly cannot do without them, but there are predators on the prowl: moles and hedgehogs are crazy about worms.

Mole, Talpa europea

Moles and hedgehogs

Everyone knows the damage which moles can do to a lawn or flower-bed. The mole hills provide the evidence. They are formed by the soil which the mole has dug up in the depths and brought up backwards. A mole hill contains at least a kilo of soil, twenty times as much as the digger's weight. It is not surprising that it has a large appetite. Every day it consumes more than its own weight in food. The meals consist almost entirely of earthworms supplemented with insect larvae, so that the mole actually also does some useful work. The hedgehog, which can even be found in small, inner-city gardens, also has two aspects. On the one hand, it feeds on worms and birds' eggs; on the other hand, on harmful caterpillars and slugs. The latter are keen plant eaters and can do a great deal of harm in the garden.

Slugs particularly manage to destroy whole leaves and fruit by scraping off the surface of a leaf or a stalk with the rasp-like sections of their mouths. The softer the material, the more popular it is with slugs, and therefore seedlings and soft fruits such as strawberries are particularly at risk. It is the hedgehog which goes on the prowl at night when slugs are active, to make short work of these greedy creatures. Hedgehogs are not very quiet; in fact they can be quite noisy and they make quite a racket when they are eating. They do not deal so successfully with snails, which are more at risk from song thrushes - beautiful birds which are found in villages and towns.

Song thrushes and blackbirds

The song thrush is one of the few creatures which has mastered the art of extracting snails from their shell. To do this it always uses the same stone as a sort of an anvil on which it smashes the snail's shell to bits. Around one of these stones - the thrush smithy - the ground is strewn with remnants of snail shells.

The blackbird has not mastered this trick. Apart from its diet of fruits and berries, it feeds on worms. It manages to lure them out of the ground by tapping on the ground with its feet in such a way that the worms think that a mole is after them and they flee up to the surface. However, a minute later they disappear down the blackbird's throat.

Song thrush, Turdus philamelos
Snail, Cepaea sp.

List of symbols

- **·** — annual
- **· ·** — biennial
- **○** — perennial
- ⬙ — bulbous plant
- ♧ — tuberous plant
- ⋇ — tree
- ⋇ — shrub
- ↕ — height in cm
- ↔ — interval between plants in cm
- ○ — full sunlight
- ◕ — semi-shade
- ● — shade
- ❀ — flowering months
- ✳ — winter-hardy
- **!** — poisonous
- ✂ — suitable for cut flowers
- ❀ — berry
- 🪣 — keep moist at all times, compost should not dry out
- 🪣 — keep moderately moist, compost may dry out slightly
- 🪣 — keep fairly dry, only water during growing period
- ⋗ — spray, avoid spraying when plant is flowering